Languages of the World

Russian

Jilly Hunt

Heinemann
LIBRARY

Chicago, Illinois

www.capstonepub.com
Visit our website to find out more information about Heinemann-Raintree books.

To order:

☎ Phone 888-454-2279

 Visit www.capstonepub.com to browse our catalog and order online.

Edited by Dan Nunn and Diyan Leake
Designed by Marcus Bell
Original illustrations © Capstone Global Library Ltd 2012
Picture research by Elizabeth Alexander

Originated by Capstone Global Library Ltd
Printed and bound in China by South China Printing
  Company Ltd

15 14 13 12 11
10 9 8 7 6 5 4 3 2 1

Library of Congress Cataloging-in-Publication Data
Hunt, Jilly.
  Russian / Jilly Hunt.—1st ed.
     p. cm.—(Languages of the world)
  Text in English and Russian.
  Includes bibliographical references and index.
  ISBN 978-1-4329-5837-4—ISBN 978-1-4329-5845-9 (pbk.)
1. Russian language—Textbooks for foreign speakers—English.
2. Russian language—Grammar. 3. Russian language—Spoken
Russian. I. Title.
  PG2129.E5H86 2012
  491.782'421—dc23   2011017926

Acknowledgments
The author and publisher are grateful to the following for permission to reproduce copyright material: Alamy pp. 7 (© Arcticphoto), 17 (© Caro), 20 (© Image Source), 21 (© Losevsky Pavel), 23 (© David White), 25 (© Imagestate Media Partners Limited—Impact Photos), 29 (© Natalya Onishchenko); Corbis p. 6 (© Peter Turnley); Getty Images pp. 22 (Kirill Kudrjavtsev/AFP), 24 (Lluis Gene/AFP); Shutterstock pp. 5 (© Liv friis-larsen), 8 (© Péter Gudella), 9 left (© Tatiana Popova), 9 middle (© fantazista), 9 right (© Utekhina Anna), 10 (© BelayaMedvedica), 11 (© Dmitriy Shironosov), 12 (© Anton Gvozdikov), 13 (© Serhiy Kobyakov), 14 (© Stephen Coburn), 15 (© Dmitriy Shironosov), 16 (© Golden Pixels LLC), 18 (© Dmitry Naumov), 19 (© krechet), 26 (© Tobik), 27 (© De Visu), 28 (© ermess).

Cover photograph eproduced with permission of Shutterstock (© Kiselev Andrey Valerevich).

Every effort has been made to contact copyright holders of material reproduced in this book. Any omissions will be rectified in subsequent printings if notice is given to the publisher.

Disclaimer
All the Internet addresses (URLs) given in this book were valid at the time of going to press. However, due to the dynamic nature of the Internet, some addresses may have changed, or sites may have changed or ceased to exist since publication. While the author and publisher regret any inconvenience this may cause readers, no responsibility for any such changes can be accepted by either the author or the publisher.

Contents

Russian words in this book are in italics, *like this*.
You can find out how to say them by looking in the
pronunciation guide.

Russian Around the World

Russian is the main language of Russia. People also speak Russian in places that used to be part of a group of countries called the Soviet Union. These countries include Belarus, Georgia, Latvia, Ukraine, Kazakhstan, Kyrgyzstan, and Moldova.

Russia

This map shows the main countries where people speak Russian.

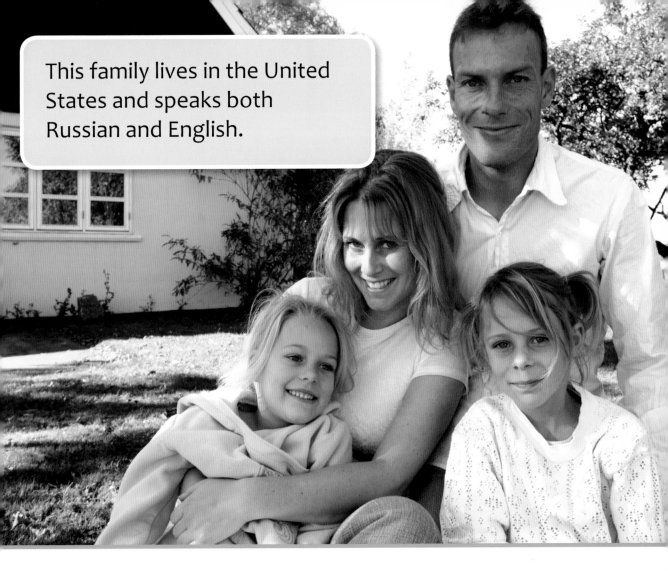

This family lives in the United States and speaks both Russian and English.

Some people also speak Russian in places where Russians have gone to live. These are places such as the United States, Canada, Israel, and Australia.

Who Speaks Russian?

More than 145 million people speak Russian as their first language. Many people also learn another language. This is called a second language. About 100 million people use Russian as their second language.

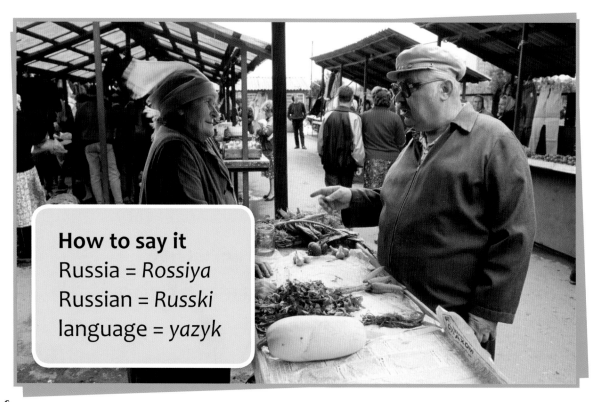

How to say it
Russia = *Rossiya*
Russian = *Russki*
language = *yazyk*

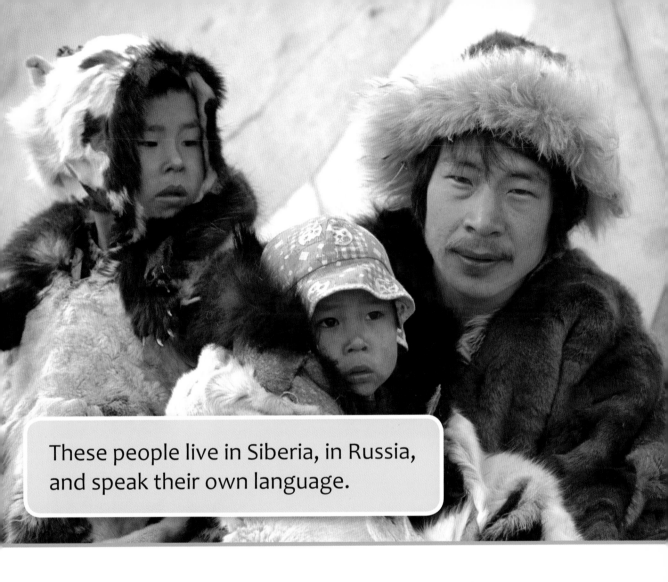

These people live in Siberia, in Russia, and speak their own language.

Russia is the biggest country in the world. There are many different regions in Russia. Some of these regions have their own languages.

Russian and English

Russian belongs to a group of languages called Slavic languages. The Russian language has borrowed some words from other languages, such as English, Greek, and French.

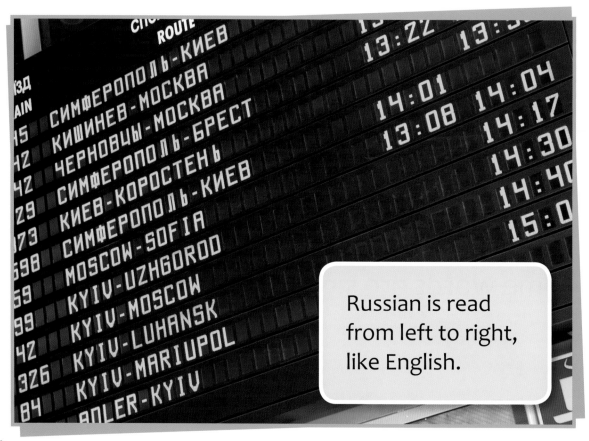

Russian is read from left to right, like English.

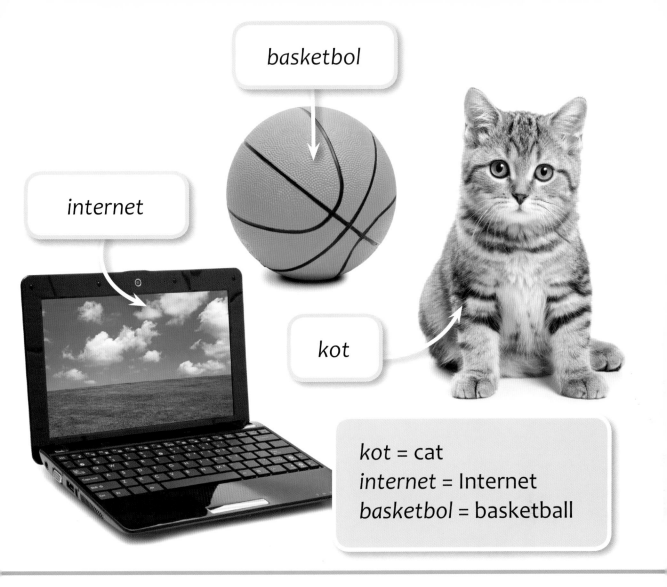

basketbol

internet

kot

kot = cat
internet = Internet
basketbol = basketball

Some words are similar in Russian and English. The Russian words for "cat," "basketball," and "Internet" sound similar to those words in English.

Learning Russian

Russian uses a different alphabet than English. It has 33 letters and is called the Cyrillic alphabet. It is based on Greek letters.

А а Б б В в Г г Д д
Е е Ё ё Ж ж З з И и
Й й К к Л л М м Н н
О о П п Р р С с Т т
У у Ф ф Х х Ц ц Ч ч
Ш ш Щ щ Ъ ъ Ы ы
Ь ь Э э Ю ю Я я

The best way to learn Russian is to listen to people speaking Russian and try to copy them.

In this book, Russian words are written in the same alphabet that is used to write English. This makes them easier for you to read.

Saying Hello and Goodbye

Russians greet each other with a hello and a handshake. Close friends greet each other with a warm hug. There are different ways to say hello to someone you don't know very well, and to a close friend.

How to say it
hello = *zdravstvuite* (to someone you don't know very well)/*privet* (to a close friend)

How to say it
goodbye = *do svidaniya* (to someone you
    don't know very well)/*poka* (to a friend)

The traditional way of saying goodbye
to family or a close friend is to give
three kisses on the cheek and a hug.

Talking About Yourself

When people meet others for the first time, they usually give their name. To tell someone your name, you might say, *"Menya zovut …"* ("My name is …")

How to say it
What is your name? = *Kak vas zovut?*
My name is Anna = *Menya zovut Anna*

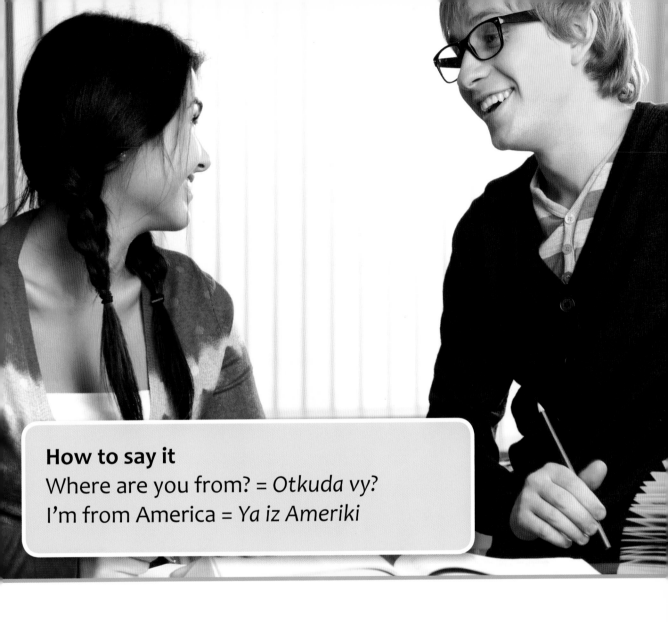

How to say it
Where are you from? = *Otkuda vy?*
I'm from America = *Ya iz Ameriki*

People often tell each other where they are from. They might say, "*Ya iz Moskvy*" ("I am from Moscow") or "*Ya iz Rossii*" ("I am from Russia").

Asking About Others

There are different ways to say "you" in Russian. Calling someone *vy* is polite. You would use this with adults. You can use *ty* for friends.

Being polite is very important to Russians.

How to say it

How are you? = *Kak dyela?*

I'm fine, thanks. And you? = *Spasibo, khorosho. A vy?*

Russians are interested in the lives of their friends. If you ask a Russian "How are you?" you may get a very full answer!

At Home

In Russia, many people live in towns and cities. Most people live in big apartment buildings. Sometimes these buildings have kitchens and bathrooms that are shared by several apartments.

How to say it
house = *dom*
apartment = *kvartira*
city = *gorod*

How to say it
village = *derevnya*
room = *komnata*
window = *okno*
door = *dver'*

In the countryside, people often live in villages. Village homes are usually bigger than those in the city. They may have their own yard.

Family Life

Families are a very important part of life in Russia. Grandparents are a special part of a Russian family. Many grandparents live with their families.

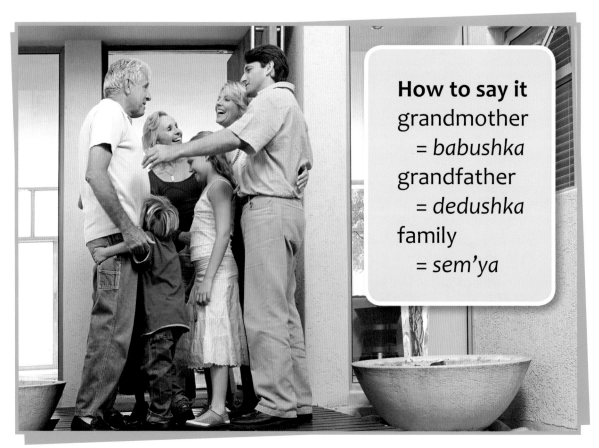

How to say it
grandmother
  = *babushka*
grandfather
  = *dedushka*
family
  = *sem'ya*

How to say it
mother = *mat'*
father = *otets*
brother = *brat*
sister = *sestra*

Many Russian families are small. They have just one or two children. Cousins, aunts, and uncles all get together at family celebrations such as birthday parties.

At School

In Russia, children can go to preschool until they are seven years old. They then go to elementary school. In school, children learn Russian, mathematics, social studies, and art.

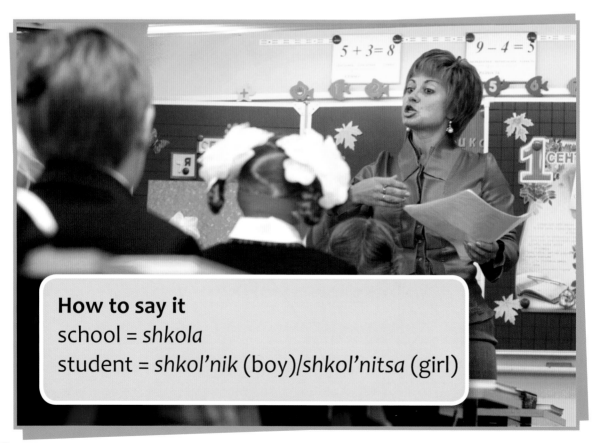

How to say it
school = *shkola*
student = *shkol'nik* (boy)/*shkol'nitsa* (girl)

How to say it
book = *kniga*
class = *klass*
teacher = *uchitel'*

Children go to school from Monday to Friday. School starts at about 8:00 a.m. and lasts until 1 or 2 p.m. Children can stay after school to do activities such as dancing or sports until 6 p.m.

Sports

Soccer is very popular in Russia. There are some great Russian soccer players. Russia will host the soccer World Cup in 2018.

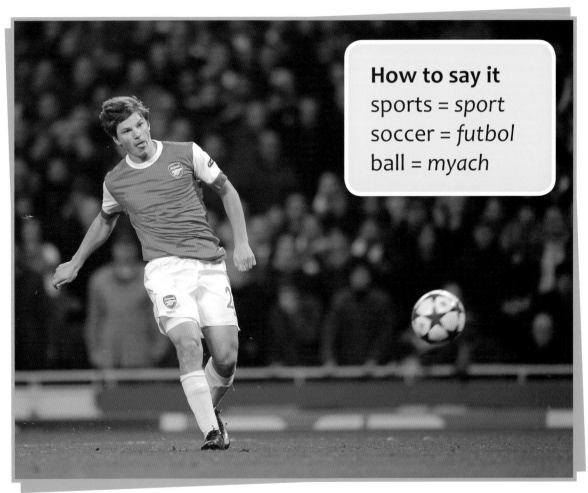

How to say it
sports = *sport*
soccer = *futbol*
ball = *myach*

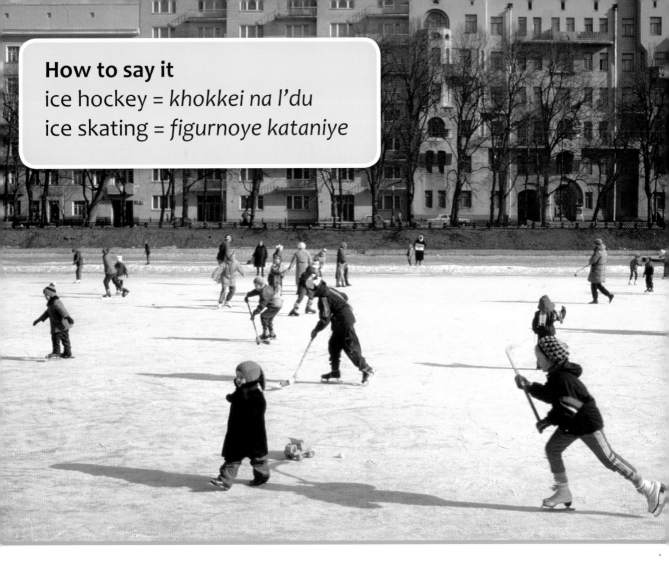

Ice hockey and basketball are also
popular sports to play in Russia.
Many people also enjoy gymnastics,
volleyball, ice skating, and chess.

Food

At home, many Russians have a big breakfast. They enjoy eating pancakes called *bliny* or porridge called *kasha*, with cottage cheese and sour cream.

How to say it
breakfast = *zavtrak*
sour cream = *smetana*

bliny

How to say it
bread = *khleb*
butter = *maslo*
bakery = *bulochnaya*

Bread is a popular part of many Russian meals, and there are many different types. A traditional type of bread is a black rye bread called *chorni* or *rzhanoi.*

Clothes

Many young Russians relax in clothes such as jeans and T-shirts. People may wear traditional clothes on special occasions, such as a festival.

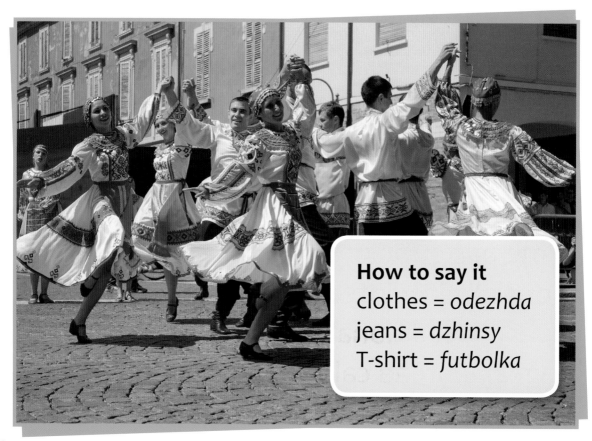

How to say it

clothes = *odezhda*

jeans = *dzhinsy*

T-shirt = *futbolka*

How to say it
coat = *pal'to*
hat = *shapka*
boots = *botinki*

Some parts of Russia get very cold,
especially in winter. In Siberia, some
people wear traditional clothes made
from animal skins to keep warm.

Pronunciation Guide

English	Russian	Pronunciation
apartment	kvartira	kvar-tee-**rah**
bakery	bulochnaya	**boo**-lahch-nah-yah
ball	myach	**myahch**
basketball	basketbol	bahs-ket-**bol**
book	kniga	**knee**-gah
boots	botinki	bah-**teen**-ki
bread	khleb	**khlep**
breakfast	zavtrak	**zahft**-rahk
brother	brat	**braht**
butter	maslo	**mahs**-lah
cat	kot	**kot**
city	gorod	**go**-raht
class	klass	**klahs**
clothes	odezhda	ah-**dezh**-dah
coat	pal'to	pahl-**to**
door	dver'	**dverr**
family	sem'ya	sem-**yah**
father	otets	ah-**tets**
goodbye	do svidaniya/poka	dah svi-**dah**-ni-yah/
grandfather	dedushka	**de**-doosh-kah
grandmother	babushka	**bah**-boosh-kah
hat	shapka	**shahp**-kah
hello	zdravstvuite/privet	**zdrah**-stvui-ti/pri-**vet**
house	dom	**dahm**
How are you?	Kak dyela?	**kahk** de-**lah**
ice hockey	khokkei na l'du	kho-**kay** nah **ldoo**

30

ice skating	*figornoye kataniye*	*fi-**goor**-nah-ye kah-tah-ni-ye*
I'm fine, thanks	*Spasibo, khorosho*	*spah-**see**-bah khah-rah-**sho***
I'm from ...	*Ya iz ...*	***yah** eez*
Internet	*internet*	*in-ter-**net***
jeans	*dzhinsy*	***jeen**-sih*
language	*yazyk*	*jah-**zeek***
mother	*mat'*	***maht***
My name is ...	*Menya zovut ...*	*me-**nyah** zah-**voot***
room	*komnata*	***kom**-nah-tah*
Russia	*Rossiya*	*rah-**see**-yah*
Russian	*Russki*	***roo**-skih*
school	*shkola*	***shko**-lah*
sister	*sestra*	*ses-**trah***
soccer	*futbol*	*foot-**bol***
sour cream	*smetana*	*sme-**tah**-nah*
sports	*sport*	***sport***
student	*shkol'nik/shkol'nitsa*	***shkol**-nik/**shkol**-ni-tsah*
T-shirt	*futbolka*	*foot-**bol**-ka*
teacher	*uchitel'* (man)	*oo-**chee**-tel/*
	uchitel'nitsa (woman)	*oo-**chee**-tel-ni-tsa*
village	*derevnya*	*de-**rev**-nyah*
What is your name?	*Kak vas zovut?*	***kahk vahs** zah-**voot***
Where are you from?	*Otkuda vy?*	*aht-**koo**-dah **vee***
window	*okno*	*ahk-**no***
yes	*da*	***dah***

*1 = odin, 2 = dva , 3 = tri, 4 = chetyre, 5 = pyat', 6 = shest', 7 = sem',
8 = vosem', 9 = dyevyat', 10 = dyesyat'*

Find Out More

Books

Amery, Healther. *The Usbourne Internet-Linked First Thousand Words in Russian*. Tulsa, Okla.: EDC, 2005.

Berge, Ann. *Russia ABCs (Country ABCs)*. Minneapolis: Picture Window, 2004.

Powell, Jillian. *Looking at Russia (Looking at Countries)*. Pleasantville, N.Y.: Gareth Stevens, 2008.

Website

http://kids.nationalgeographic.com/kids/places/find/russia

Index